Kids in Tune

by Nancy Vogel

Modern Curriculum Press

Credits

Photos: All photos © Pearson Learning unless otherwise noted.
Front cover, Title page, 5: Steve Ferry for Pearson Learning. 6, 7, 8, 9: Courtesy of
Tampa Bay Children's Chorus. 11, 12: Steve Ferry for Pearson Learning. 13: Courtesy
of Tampa Bay Children's Chorus. 14: Steve Ferry for Pearson Learning. 15, 16:
Courtesy of Tampa Bay Children's Chorus. 17, 18, 19: Steve Ferry for Pearson
Learning. 20: David Young-Wolff/PhotoEdit. 21: Steve Ferry for Pearson Learning. 22,
23: Courtesy of Tampa Bay Children's Chorus.

Cover and book design by Stephen Barth

ISBN 0-7652-1364-8

Printed in the United States of America
4 5 6 7 8 9 10 11   07 06 05 04 03 02

Modern Curriculum Press

Pearson Learning Group

1-800-321-3106
www.pearsonlearning.com

Contents

To Rory and B.J., who like to sing

Chapter 1
Singing Everywhere

Sing songs! See other towns, states, and countries! The children who belong to the Tampa Bay Children's Chorus get to do all of these things and more.

Children enjoy singing in the TBCC.

Many children from the Tampa area sing in the TBCC.

A chorus is a group of people who sing together. The people who belong to the Tampa Bay Children's Chorus, or TBCC, are children. All of the singers are 7 to 17 years old. They live in and around Tampa, Florida.

The TBCC members do much of their singing around Tampa. They also sing in other places in Florida.

Some of the children travel to big cities to sing. They have gone to New York City and Washington, D.C. They have even traveled to other countries to sing. A few of these countries are Canada, France, and Austria.

Chorus members stop for lunch in Austria.

The TBCC was started in 1989 by Dr. Averill Summer. She loved to hear children sing. She knew other people did, too.

Dr. Summer also wanted children to learn the very best music. Some of the music she chose was written by Johann Sebastian Bach and Wolfgang Amadeus Mozart. These men lived long ago. They wrote beautiful music that people still like listening to today.

Dr. Averill Summer with two chorus members

Two chorus members work on a skit at a music camp.

Many children wanted to be in Dr. Summer's singing group. The children who were picked for the chorus worked hard to learn the music. They also became good friends.

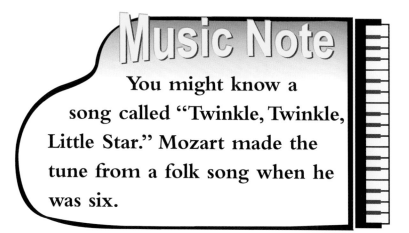

Music Note

You might know a song called "Twinkle, Twinkle, Little Star." Mozart made the tune from a folk song when he was six.

Chapter 2

Join the Group

Every year the chorus invites new singers to join the TBCC. Signs that say "Singers Needed" are put up all over the city. The signs invite children from the Tampa Bay area to come to an audition.

A poster tells about chorus auditions.

The director sings with children at an audition.

The leader of the chorus is called the director. First the director asks, "What song do you want to sing?" Then the director invites each child to sing.

It's OK if someone cannot think of a song. If this happens, the director asks, "Would you like to sing 'Happy Birthday'?"

Each child sings a song at an audition.

As each child sings, the director listens. Then the child and the director sing together. When they are finished, the director might say to the child, "You have a wonderful singing voice."

Dr. Summer with directors and new chorus member

The children who have the best singing voices are asked to join the chorus. They are very happy. They know there will be a lot of work and fun to come.

Music Note

When the director and a child sing together, they might sing a round. One singer sings the first line. Then the second singer starts the first line.

Chapter 3

Practice, Practice!

A new singer in the TBCC joins one of four groups. The youngest singers are seven years old. Next are the eight and nine year olds. There are two older groups, too. After the new members are chosen, the chorus begins to practice.

The youngest group practices a new song.

The older singers have fun at music camp.

The older children begin their practice together by going on a trip. Just before school begins, they go to a camp for a weekend. They get to know each other. They play games and sing.

During the day special teachers help the children with their singing. In the evenings the children learn fun dances. They also enjoy putting on skits.

15

The children learn many different songs. A song may have special parts. A part for one singer is called a solo. A part for two singers is called a duet. Solos or duets may be one line of a song or a whole song.

A chorus member sings a solo.

The chorus practices taking a bow.

Children work hard to learn their parts in the songs. That's not all they have to learn before they are ready to sing for others. They also have to learn where to stand and how to walk on and off the stage. Just as they do in school, they have to practice.

Music Note

TBCC singers practice once a week. The youngest group practices for one hour. The oldest group practices for two hours.

Chapter 4
On Stage

Getting ready for a show can be exciting and scary. There is so much to remember. The singers have to remember what to sing, when to sing, and where to stand.

A singer's mom helps her get ready.

The chorus warms up.

Everyone gathers 45 minutes before the show. Names are called. Clothes are checked.

Then the chorus warms up their voices. They sing notes. They wiggle their bodies, too. This helps the singers get ready for the show.

People clap for the singers.

Then the children hear the notes on the piano. The children walk out onto the stage. The chorus bursts into song.

Everyone smiles as they listen. People clap after each song. Sometimes people cheer at the end of a show. This makes the children smile, too.

If there is time, the people who have seen the show meet the chorus. The children like to talk about their singing.

Some shows are close to home. The chorus sings for special parties. They also sing for big sports games and other children. Groups of older people love to hear the children sing, too.

People like to meet the singers after the show.

Some shows are far from home.
When children are 11, they can go on
singing tours to many places.

After they get back, the children have
a lot of stories to tell. One singer may
talk about singing in France. Another
may tell about seeing a waterfall in
Canada. A third may tell about the
people she met in England.

The TBCC sings at a sports event.

Chorus members meet people after a
show in Austria.

The children in the TBCC love to
sing and make new friends. People
around the world love to hear them
sing, too.

Music Note

In 1994 the TBCC sang
with children from Finland,
Canada, and England in the
All-World Children's Choir.

Glossary

audition   [aw DIH shun] a tryout to show one's skill

chorus   [KOR us] a group of singers

director   [duh REK tur] the conductor, or leader, of a musical group

duet   [doo ET] a song or part of a song sung by two people

note   [noht] a single sound made by an instrument or voice

practice   [PRAK tus] do something over and over to do it well

solo   [SOH loh] a song or part of a song sung by one person

tour   [TOOR] a trip to perform in different places